The Sandbags and the Fire

How Leaders Cut Loose Their Hang-ups & Soar to Success

By
Scott Greenberg

Jump Start Performance Programs
PO Box 3448
Van Nuys, CA 91407

Cover Design by Becky Neiman
Layout by Jo Packham
Edited by Debi Huang

ISBN: 1-893962-02-4

For additional copies, please call 1-800-450-0432. Quantity discounts available.

Printed in the United States

TABLE OF CONTENTS:

INTRODUCTION
CUT LOOSE YOUR SANDBAGS

SECTION #1: THE SANDBAGS

1. THE MENTAL HECKLER
Managing Negative Self-Talk

2. FEAR
False Expectations Appearing Real

3. OLD INSECURITIES
Update Your Self-Image

4. TAKING THE EASY WAY
Step Outside Your Comfort Zone

5. FITTING IN
Dare to be Different

6. "IF ONLY..." & "I SHOULD..."
Being Who You Are With What You Have

7. PLEASING OTHERS
Overcome Your Image

8. AVOIDING CONFRONTATION
Stop Backing Down & Start Standing Up

9. NEGATIVE PEOPLE
Do Your Friends Pump You Up or Keep You Down?

10. CHANGING PEOPLE
Accept or Exit

11. RESISTING CHANGE
Going With a New Flow

12. IMPATIENCE
Take a Chill!

13. MOVING TOO SLOW
Take Action!

SECTION #2: THE FIRE

1. INCREASING YOUR PERSONAL POWER
Be the Best You

2. TAKING RISKS
Living on the Edge Without Falling Off

3. BE A JUDGE, NOT A SUSPECT
Don't Worry About What Others Think – YOU Do the Thinking!

4. GO FOR THE GOALS YOU CONTROL
Do What You Can, and Forget About the Rest

5. FOCUS ON FACTS, NOT ON FEELINGS
How to Tell the Difference Between a Problem and an Insecurity

6. BEATING THE COMPETITION
How to Fly Right Past 'Em

7. SET YOUR SIGHTS ON YOUR STRENGTHS
Let Your Greatness Lift You Up

INTRODUCTION

You were built for flight. You were designed to soar to the highest heights and to do great things. You are strong, powerful and aerodynamic. Your success is absolutely possible. Yet, you sometimes find yourself on the ground going nowhere. Or maybe you're hovering slightly above ground, looking to the skies, scratching your head, wondering how to move upward. You ponder what's wrong with you. What are you not doing? Where do you fall short? Why aren't you more successful?

You do not lack talent, ability or intelligence. You're not missing something. It's all there. That's not the problem. The problem is your sandbags.

As you pursue your ascent to success, you are weighed down by a number of behaviors, beliefs and circumstances. I call these limitations "sandbags." Some come from conditions out of your control. Those we won't worry about. If we did, it would cause us to blame others, blame life and surrender our power. Circumstances out of our control are normal turbulence. They make our flight a little bumpy, but they can't stop our ascent.

We're going to focus on the sandbags you've tied on yourself. The ones you control. The problems you can do something about.

Fortunately, you also have "fire," the force that propels you upward. There are behaviors and habits – choices you can make – that will launch you toward success.

In the follow pages I'm going to discuss the most common ways we hold ourselves back. I'll also offer tips to accelerate you toward your goals. In each chapter, relate the material to your own life, and brainstorm how you can apply what you read to your own flight plan.

This is powerful stuff with proven results. The question isn't will this material work for you. The question is, will *you* work for you?

Scott Greenberg

CUT LOOSE YOUR SANDBAGS
By
Scott Greenberg

If you're weighed down by fear, cut it loose.
If you're weighed down by anger, cut it loose.
If you're weighed down by hatred, cut it loose.
If you're weighed down by stress, cut it loose.
If you're weighed down by insecurity, cut it loose.
If you're weighed down by greed, cut it loose.
If you're weighed down by ambition, cut it loose.
If you're weighed down by guilt, cut it loose.
If you're weighed down by shame, cut it loose.
If you're weighed down by self-doubt, cut it loose.
If you're weighed down by worry, cut it loose.
If you're weighed down by a bad habit, cut it loose.
If you're weighed down by ignorance, cut it loose.
If you're weighed down by apathy, cut it loose.
If you're weighed down by your image, cut it loose.
If you're weighed down by needing to be right, cut it lose.
If you're weighed down by prejudice, cut it loose.
If you're weighed down by unrequited love, cut it loose.
If you're weighed down by a bad memory, cut it loose.
If you're weighed down by embarrassment, cut it loose.
If you're weighed down by inflexibility, cut it loose.
If you're weighed down by failure, cut it loose.
If you're weighed down by poor health, cut it loose.
If you're weighed down by immorality, cut it loose.
If you're weighed down by what other people think, cut it loose.
If you're weighed down by expectations, cut them loose.
If you're weighed down by a bad mate, cut him or her loose.
If you're weighed down by unhealthy friends, cut them loose.
If you're weighted down by too many commitments, cut them loose.

What sandbags are keeping you down?

SECTION #1: **The Sandbags**

THE MENTAL HECKLER
Managing Negative Self-Talk

In my presentations, I often talk about the "mental heckler," referring to the voice in your head that often criticizes you and makes you feel bad about yourself. I'm not talking about your conscience, your basic thoughts or even a positive voice that encourages you. I'm talking about that little cynic that says things like "You're too fat" or "That person would never go out with you" or "You sounded so ridiculous in that meeting." This voice is one way you may be sandbagging yourself. I devote a lot of time to studying this voice and learning how to manage it. The better we cope with negative self-talk, the greater our chances of maximizing our potential.

Here are a few tips to manage your mental heckler:

1. DON'T TRY TO SILENCE THE VOICE. Telling the mental heckler to shut up will only make it talk louder. I was once at an NBA game and watched some fans harassing one of the players. The player got angry and responded. The fans, delighted to be acknowledged, only made it worse for him. The best athletes are able to focus on their game, regardless of what is being said around them or to them. To manage the nasty fan in your head, try to disregard it completely. To do this, you too must focus on what you are trying to accomplish.

2. DON'T STOP TO EVALUATE YOURSELF WHILE IN THE MIDDLE OF SOMETHING. If you do this during a rough time, you'll awaken the mental heckler. Again, stay focused.

3. TRUST YOURSELF. Most of us perform at our best naturally. Thinking too much interferes. Getting back to the basketball example, most NBA stars will tell you that while playing, they don't think much about technique or the mechanics of shooting. They just envision the ball going into the basket and let their body do what it's supposed to do. Thinking too much about the "how to's" will lead to discouragement as you notice your mistakes. Your instincts are better than you realize. Trust your abilities and avoid entertaining self-doubt.

4. WRITE DOWN WHAT THE MENTAL HECKLER SAYS. Getting those thoughts out of your head and onto paper allows you to clear your mind and look at your circumstances more objectively. Often when you read on paper what the heckler is saying, you'll find its comments are totally ridiculous.

5. DISCUSS YOUR NEGATIVE VOICE WITH SOMEONE ELSE. Sometimes articulating what it says out loud puts everything in perspective. You'll also benefit from the reaction of the person you're talking to. Our friends are great resources for helping us with insecurity.

6. KNOW THAT THE MENTAL HECKLER CARES. We get insecure and live in fear because we want to protect ourselves from getting hurt. By stopping you from taking risks and pursuing goals, the voice safeguards you from failure. It also stops you from success. Remind the heckler (and yourself) that you are willing to endure occasional suffering to achieve your goals.

7. JUST BE AWARE. Simply knowing that you have this voice – and that it's not necessarily correct – may be enough. It's OK to be insecure. What's not OK is letting insecurity stop you from taking action. Be aware of the voice, but know you don't have to listen.

Your mind is your greatest obstacle. The mental heckler serves as a distraction. Focusing on your goals and what you must do to achieve them will distract you from this distraction, freeing you to take action.

FEAR
False Expectations Appearing Real

Many of us are plagued by fear. We stress, we worry, we freak out. We play the "What if?" game in our head, obsessing over worst-case scenarios. The funny thing is, rarely do our fears become reality. In fact, we spend a lot more time worrying than we do experiencing real problems. Maybe the fear is actually the worst problem we face.

Someone once told me the letters that make up the word "fear" stand for False Expectations Appearing Real. Things are fine, but we believe there's a problem. That belief itself is the true problem. And it makes us do crazy things.

For example, when I was young I had a fear of going to bed at night with my closet door open. I was afraid that if I fell asleep and my closet was even slightly open, in the middle of the night, this big horrible monster was going to burst out, tear me apart and steal my blanket! No matter how comfy I was in bed, I always got up to close the closet. What was even sillier was my belief that this horrible monster couldn't reopen the door himself from the inside! It's a ridiculous belief. But that's how fear works.

It's difficult to rid yourself of fear. But that's not what's important. What's important is that you don't let fear hold you back.

Not long ago I was cast as a co-host for the pilot episode of a reality television show in Los Angeles. My role entailed taking couples through a ropes course and facilitating discussion -- stuff I do all the time. However, when I got on location and saw the lights, cameras and TV executives, I heard that inner voice telling me I was in way over my head. "What was I doing there? Who was I to work in television? I should quit right now". I even called my wife and expressed my self-doubt. Too late to turn back, I plunged in, as I would a cold swimming pool.

When the time finally came to perform on camera, I nervously stuttered through the word "facilitator." One of the producers shouted "cut!" and sarcastically explained how the word "facilitator" is pronounced in the English language. I responded explaining that as the "artist" on set, I should be able to "interpret" my lines any way I want and that he should stick to producing. Everyone on set laughed at our exchange and suddenly the mood lightened. I stopped thinking so much about my performance and just did my job. The shoot went very well and I received big-time kudos from the producers. As usual, the cynical voice in my head was wrong. The pilot never turned into a real television show (not many do), but the experience was a wonderful way to confirm my abilities and invalidate my fears.

We are all more capable than we realize. While we can't always avoid fear and self-doubt, we do have self-control. Push yourself forward as often as you can. Don't let insecurity stop you from experiencing your full potential.

If you're going to play the "What if?" game, finish it. Consider what will actually happen if your fear becomes a reality. Will it be that bad? Will you really be unable to handle it? Many times even the worst-case scenario isn't so bad.

Confront your fears, and take action in spite of them. The more you do this, the less fear you'll have.

OLD INSECURITIES
Update Your Self-Image

Brandy was awkward when she was a kid. She had big, wild hair, was on the taller side and always felt like she didn't fit in. When it seemed like all her friends were dating, Brandy rarely, if ever, got asked out. By the time high school ended, her only date was a guy friend she asked to the prom. By her own standards, Brandy was a nerd.

Things changed in college. She got her hair under control. She matured and discovered her strengths. Guys started asking her out. She had new friends. It was a totally difference experience from high school, and Brandy came into her own.

The only thing that didn't change was Brandy's self-image. Though life was totally different, Brandy still saw herself as a nerd. No amount of success, popularity or attention from guys could change her perception of herself. It was as if her feelings from her younger years were permanently branded on her brain. Today, well into her thirties, Brandy, whom everyone else loves and admires, refuses to see herself as anything other than the tall, big-haired dork from high school.

Many of us see ourselves today the way we were many years ago. Though our childhood and teen years represent only a fraction of our lives, that seems to be when we lock onto our self-image.

We can't permanently define ourselves because we are always growing and changing. In my presentations I sometimes use the analogy of a pancake that's only half cooked. It needs more time, and so might you. Who you were five years ago is not who you are today. And today's you will be different five years from now.

A great way to prove this point is to go on the Internet and find pictures of today's successful people when they were teenagers. You'll be blown away by how many amazing people were once awkward. Funny thing is, many of these people still see themselves as dorks.

We all grow at our own pace. While you may not fit in with today's "normal" group, you may be the leader of tomorrow's.

TAKING THE EASY WAY
Step Outside Your Comfort Zone

We humans love to be comfortable. We stay where we feel safe. We stick to the same routine. We develop habits based on what we know. The problem is, when we do things by instinct, we forget we have choices. That holds us back. If you keep doing what you're doing, you'll keep getting what you're getting. To grow, you must expose yourself to something new, and possibly, uncomfortable.

Remember your first day of school? If you were like me, you might have cried. I wanted to stay home with my mom where things were familiar. But like all kids, I was forced to go. The first hour or so was terrifying. Everything was new, different and therefore, quite scary. I was uncomfortable, to say the least.

But it didn't stay that way long. After my eyes dried I started to look around and got a feel for kindergarten. I learned how to raise my hand, and where the bathroom was. They showed us where to find the paint and where to put our lunch boxes. The teacher smiled a lot and called me by my name. The playground was awesome! I enjoyed the new friends I made and the games we got to play. School wasn't as bad as I thought!

Within a few hours of being outside my comfort zone, my comfort zone started to expand. Suddenly school felt safe. By the end of the first day, I didn't want to leave.

Every new experience is like our first day of school. We resist it out of fear and discomfort. Once we jump in, it becomes OK.

Spend some time noticing your habits and where you cling to what's comfortable. For example, try clasping your hands together. Notice which thumb is on top. Now, clasp your hands the other way, with the other thumb on top. How's that feel? Probably pretty uncomfortable. Still, one way is not more correct than the other. It's just more familiar.

Comfort keeps us grounded, but it also stops us from moving forward. By pushing yourself beyond what feels safe and familiar, you'll increase your personal power. Try new things and get more experience. Eventually, the hard stuff will become much easier.

FITTING IN
Dare to be Different

When I was a little kid, it was popular to wear Ocean Pacific ("OP") corduroy shorts. They were cut pretty short, exposing a small birthmark I have on the back of my left thigh. Because of that birthmark, I always felt inadequate and different. I felt like damaged goods and didn't fit in. These feelings were reinforced by other differences I had, such as being Jewish and living in a house where we always took off our shoes. No matter how hard I tried, somehow I just never felt normal. I was quite self-conscious.

Today these differences still exist. Fortunately I no longer feel different; I feel special. I've learned not only to accept myself, but to feel proud of the things that distinguish me from others. Our society doesn't reward people for fitting in. It's those who stand out who get the recognition.

Life is not about being like everyone else as much as it is about being OK with who you are. You'll never be the best you possible by pretending to be something you're not. Instead of hiding your differences, celebrate them! Flaunt them! Your differences are what make you unique. They give you identity. They're what separate you from the pack.

And the truth is, no one is "normal." I recently asked a group of about 100 high school students to raise their hand if they sometimes feel like they don't fit in. Almost everyone raised their hand. No matter how confident and ordinary others may seem, on the inside, they too have the feelings I had when I was a kid. To some extent, everyone feels different (even if they pretend not to). Those who don't are actually in the minority.

Get to know yourself and feel good about your unique qualities. You are special, and any friend worth having will appreciate you exactly as you are.

"IF ONLY..." & "I SHOULD..."
Being Who You Are With
What You Have

Often we blame our unhappiness on "if only's." "If only I had more money..." "If only I lived somewhere else..." "If only I was skinnier..." We say "if only" as if we've been done some great injustice.

This is a victim mentality. You are strong, powerful and creative. You already have all the resources you need to be successful, or the means to get these resources. When you wish your circumstances were different, you give up your personal power. We can't control the "if only's." But we do have a say over the action we take. Focus on what you can do, who you already are and what you already have.

Another sandbag phrase is "I should." "I should work harder..." "I should look a certain way..." "I should be kinder..." And on and on. Thinking "I should" is very disempowering. It makes us feel guilty. It invalidates what we're already doing. And often we say "I should" for the wrong reasons. For example, when you feel you should dress a certain way, why should you? Is it because it'll make you happier? Or, is it because others say so? When you think "I should," examine your motivation. Are you acting out of a desire to better yourself, or to please others? The only thing you should do is what's right for you.

In no way am I advocating being irresponsible, breaking the law or dishonoring those who look out for you. Taking good advice and working within agreed-upon structures often sets us up for success. But be aware of when "I should's" hold you back. You always have choices. The more options you see, the more power you have.

PLEASING OTHERS
Overcome Your Image

We spend a lot of time worrying about what people think. We place a high value on our popularity, image and reputation. There's nothing wrong with wanting respect, until your desire to please others becomes so strong that you sacrifice your own identity.

In one of my presentations, I ask audience members to share examples of things they've done to impress others, or things they have not done because they've been afraid of what people would think. The responses I get amaze me. Young people choose and resist friends based on who can promote their reputation. Adults drive cars they can't afford. People hide their true feelings, develop eating disorders, succumb to peer pressure. Some act wild and outrageous to stand out. Some keep silent to fit in. Some people completely hide their true personality. It goes beyond wanting to be seen as "normal" by society. It becomes an obsession.

No matter how hard we try, we will never impress everyone. Fortunately, we don't need to. If you truly want to be happy, the only one you have to please is yourself. The most powerful you is the most authentic you. The more real you can be, the more strength you will have. We think that if we act a certain way, it'll make people like us. Actually, the opposite is true. By not acting – by being ourselves – we maximize our appeal.

Imagine never having to worry about impressing people. What would that feel like? What would be possible for you? What would you be able to do? When you stop trying to please others, you will be set free.

AVOIDING CONFRONTATION
Stop Backing Down &
Start Standing Up

Sometimes people in our lives do things we don't like. In many cases, their behavior doesn't directly impact us. Other times, however, people do things that directly cause us harm. In these instances, we have every right to confront them about their behavior. But you don't have to cause a fight! With some finesse and a little assertiveness, your feedback can be constructive. Here's how to do it:

1. ASK QUESTIONS. Before expressing your dissatisfaction, find out more about why the person is doing what they're doing. They may have an explanation you're not aware of that will change your feelings.

2. BE ASSERTIVE AND DIRECT, BUT NOT ANGRY. This means you may have to wait until you're calm and collected. Avoid letting emotion hinder your ability to communicate well.

3. MAINTAIN EYE CONTACT. This may be uncomfortable during a confrontation, but it tells the person you're serious. It's also a good idea to be on the same physical level, so you're not looking up or down at the person you're confronting.

4. COMMENT ON THE BEHAVIOR, NOT THE PERSON. Don't name-call or make any broad, negative comments about someone's personality. Insulting people only makes them defensive. Comment only on what the person has been doing. Let the person know how his or her behavior affects you and how it makes you feel. The person may not have realized the impact of his or her actions. Sharing your feelings lets the person know why it's appropriate for you to say something. (We all have the right to defend ourselves!)

5. USE THE "WHEN YOU, I FEEL..." FORMULA. Use this phrase to clearly describe your problem. For example, "When you interrupt me, I feel like my thoughts aren't important."

6. FOCUS ONLY ON ONE BEHAVIOR. Don't turn the conversation into a free-for-all critique session. Keep your comments specific to the item of contention.

7. STICK TO YOUR GUNS. You can be wrong about the facts, but you can't be wrong about your feelings. Don't let the discomfort of the confrontation scare you away.

8. MAKE A REQUEST. Don't just criticize what the person is doing. Suggest actions you can take together to resolve the situation.

9. EXPRESS APPRECIATION FOR THE PERSON'S WILLINGNESS TO LISTEN. That'll soften the moment and minimize the sting of criticism.

Remember that confrontation isn't always easy, but it's an important part of any healthy relationship. People who care about you can't take your feelings into consideration unless you express them.

NEGATIVE PEOPLE
Do Your Friends Pump You Up, or Keep You Down?

I played tennis in high school and was told early on to play people who were better than me. (Trust me, it wasn't hard to find an opponent.) The idea is that when you're around a good player, it brings out the best in you. I've since learned this is also a great way to choose friends.

There are two kinds of people in our lives – Energizers and Dead Batteries. Energizers make us feel great about ourselves. They remind us of how good we are. They motivate us and generally make us feel better just by being around.

Then there are the Dead Batteries. These are the people who drain us of energy. They complain and they discourage. Or maybe they don't do anything in particular, but for some reason, they just make us feel bad.

I used to have a good friend whom I really couldn't count on. He was a lot of fun. But he'd also be extremely flaky and unreliable. Often we'd make plans, and he'd cancel at the last minute. It was one of those friendships that had to be forced along (where you feel a bit taken for granted). When I left him a message telling him I was getting married, I didn't hear from him for almost a month. That made me realize that this friendship led to a lot more disappointments than good times. There wasn't a problem here to be fixed. It was just who he was. I had to answer a tough question. Did this friend contribute to my life, or take away from it? The disappointments far outweighed the good times, and I've let the friendship fade away. It was hard, but I feel it was the right decision.

Because the people around us have a tremendous influence on our lives, it is crucial that you surround yourself with Energizers. Every person in your life should somehow improve you. Dead Batteries should be cut loose. There's absolutely no reason why you should have to endure anyone who doesn't make you feel good. Sometimes this is a hard thing to do. But have faith. Your life WILL improve by keeping positive people around you.

CHANGING PEOPLE
Accept or Exit

My college roommate was the messiest human being I've ever met. His life was one large pile. I could never tell how he sorted his dirty laundry from the clean, or if he even bothered. His closet emitted odors that would perplex a hazardous materials team. And when it came to cleaning up common areas, he and I had totally different standards. For example, when we'd run out of clean plates, I'd suggest we do the dishes. He would suggest we buy more.

As the months ticked by, my frustration increased. We would have "roommate meetings" to discuss his habits, but he'd never change his ways, even when he agreed to. After six months, we had a blowout. Then we didn't speak for almost two weeks. Finally, there was a change – me. I gave up hoping my roommate would develop new habits. Instead I backed off and accepted his lifestyle. The mess never disappeared, but the tension did.

I've learned that it's impossible to change a person. You can encourage new behaviors, but ultimately it's up to people to change themselves. As outsiders, all we can do is accept people or choose not to be with them.

The truth is, there was a lot more to my roommate than his messiness. He was a loyal friend, a great listener and a lot of fun to be around. Accepting his mess was really a small price to pay to enjoy everything else that made him cool.

But sometimes, the price to maintain a relationship is too high. For example, you can't stop someone from being abusive (to others or to themselves). While you can hope they'll rehabilitate themselves, there's no way to know for sure if or when this will happen. And you have no power to make it happen. All you can do is protect yourself, and that may mean leaving the relationship.

Before making any hasty decisions, ask yourself why the person's behavior bothers you. Is what they're doing wrong, or is it just different from how you would do it? Sometimes when people have different ways of doing things, it can rub you the wrong way. However, your approach may be no more correct. (Who's to say how neat the dorm room should be?) Perhaps you just need to compromise.

In other instances, people may not realize their behavior directly impacts you. If the behavior isn't already ingrained into their identity, they may be able to change. You just have to respectfully let them know how you feel. If, after a few attempts their behavior remains the same, chances are they're not going to change.

We must love people for who they are, not what we want them to be. Accepting people as they are will relieve you of the stress that comes with trying to change them. Leaving unacceptable people will relieve you of the stress that comes with trying to stay.

RESISTING CHANGE
Going With a New Flow

There's an awesome book called "Who Moved My Cheese?" by Spencer Johnson, M.D. (Putnam Publishing Group, September 1998). It's about lab mice that live in a maze. Every day they take the same path to get to the cheese. One day the cheese is moved. One mouse is prepared to deal with this change. Another continues along the usual path, unable to accept that the cheese is no longer in the same spot.

The one thing we can count on in our lives is change. Your ability to deal with change is critical. Corporate America spends millions of dollars a year training employees to adapt to new situations. Those who can't, get left behind, or, as Spencer Johnson might say, run out of cheese.

Here are a few things you can do to prepare yourself for change:

1. DON'T RELY TOO HEAVILY ON YOUR CURRENT CIRCUMSTANCES.

2. DON'T MAKE LONG-TERM COMMITMENTS YOU CAN'T HANDLE.

3. SAVE YOUR MONEY FOR A "RAINY DAY."

4. BRAINSTORM "WHAT IF'S," AND THEN DEVELOP BACK UP PLANS. A good plan "B" will make you feel more secure about plan "A."

5. EMBRACE CHANGE. There's a fine line between stability and stasis. Sometimes we need change to set us free of our limitations.

6. NETWORK LIKE CRAZY. Cultivate and maintain relationships. You may need them down the line.

7. BELIEVE YOU'LL LAND ON YOUR FEET. No matter what happens, you're going to be OK. Have faith in yourself.

IMPATIENCE
Take a Chill!

As a kid, I used to make model airplanes. They never turned out right. I never had the patience to let the glue dry adequately before moving on to the next step. Invariably the model would fall apart. Since then, I've been in a lot of situations when I've jumped the gun. I've spoken without thinking. I've made impulse purchases I couldn't afford. Worst of all, I've tried to find solutions while still freaked out by problems.

There have been other times when I've been rewarded for my patience. I'll never forget the start of the Los Angeles Marathon. When they fired the gun, thousands of competitive runners took off like bullets across the starting line. They were so eager to get a head start that they burned a lot of energy during the first few miles. As I reached mile 12, I saw many of these same people – walking. My pace was slow and steady. In spite of a knee injury, I came in ahead of two-thirds of the runners.

I learned that long distance running is less about running fast than it is about running smart.

As leaders we are told to take action. While I believe this is important, I'm starting to learn that knowing when to remain still can be equally effective. Often we try too hard, do too much and wind up repelling success. Knowing when to be patient allows you to proceed intelligently. By taking action, you plant seeds that will pay off later. However, many of these seeds cannot be rushed to growth. You must give them time to germinate.

My favorite book is James Clavell's classic novel, *Shogun* (Dell Publishing Company, June 1976). One of the main characters in the book is a wise Japanese governor named Toranaga. When war becomes increasingly imminent, everyone pressures Toranaga to act. But he refuses. His philosophy is that with patience and time, the answers will present themselves. I won't spoil the ending should you wish to read it. But let's just say his patience pays off.

So how do you know when to be still and when to take action? If you can be productive and calm, proceed. But if your primary motivation is impatience, or if you're feeling urgency, there's a good chance that taking a little time away from the situation will allow you to evaluate things more clearly and perform more effectively.

Some say there's no better time than the present. I say, there's no better present than time.

MOVING TOO SLOW
Take Action!

In the last chapter we looked at the power of patience. While it's important to proceed cautiously, sometimes waiting too long will kill an opportunity.

My junior year in high school I was class president. I was in charge of planning the prom. I took care of every detail except for one – getting my own date. I hesitated, thinking it was too early to ask the person I wanted. (After all, I didn't want to look overeager.) Before I knew it, she already had a date. When the prom came around, there was no one to take. Hours before the dance, I learned a female friend wasn't going either. By default, we went together. It was far from what I had envisioned for my prom.

When you know what you want, don't let fear, passivity or laziness (the three biggest reasons for procrastinating) cause you to delay. Take immediate action. When I moved to New York, I got an amazing apartment because I was the first person to answer the ad.

There's a difference between acting impulsively and acting swiftly. When you're impulsive, you act without thinking. Being swift means you think, decide and act without hesitation.

There are other people who want the same things you do. The sooner you take action, the greater your chances of success.

SECTION #2: **The Fire**

INCREASING YOUR PERSONAL POWER
Be the Best You

Although I write, coach and speak for a living, I think of myself less as a teacher and more as a student. When I speak, I'm really just giving a book report. I'm always reading, watching and asking questions. It really makes a difference for me not only as a speaker, but also as an ambitious person. I've learned that leadership is a dynamic process. The best leaders actively seek self-improvement because they know personal power isn't permanent. Like the cliché says, "If you snooze, you lose."

Fortunately, it doesn't take much to keep you on top of your game. I recommend devoting 15 minutes a day to your leadership development. If you do that on a regular basis, I'll guarantee you'll feel significant growth. Nurture your development as a leader by:

-Listening to tapes.
-Reading books.
-Checking out self-improvement Web
  sites.
-Attending classes and conferences.
-Starting leadership discussion groups.
-Subscribing to leadership newsletters.
-Watching people and journaling about
  your observations.
-Watching YOURSELF and journaling
  about your observations.

When we exercise our bodies, we become physically stronger. Actively develop your leadership skills and you'll be surprised how quickly you build up your personal power and influence.

TAKING RISKS
Living on the Edge Without Falling Off

I'll never forget my first speech. I was running for vice-president in fifth grade. I had to get up in front of hundreds of students. Everyone would be watching me. The potential for humiliation was great. What if I forgot my speech? What if I fell off the stage? And as if giving a speech wasn't scary enough, I was going to attempt to lead a cheer. What if no one participated? I'd look like an idiot!

Everything I've ever accomplished in my life was a result of taking some kind of risk. Unless we put ourselves out there, we have no chance to succeed. There's no way to ever guarantee success. But there is one way to guarantee failure, and that's by not even trying.

It is true that when you set out to accomplish something, there's a chance you'll fail, get rejected and maybe even embarrass yourself. Most successful people can recite all kinds of stories about times when things went wrong for them. They'll also tell you it was worth it because of all the other times they've prevailed. The rewards almost always outweigh the failures.

You can't avoid nervous feelings, but you can manage them. Here are some techniques I've learned to help me when taking a risk:

1. DON'T THINK TOO MUCH. The easiest way to get into a cold swimming pool is to jump right in. The same can be said for taking risks. Hesitating will only psyche you out.

2. WHEN YOU JUMP, JUMP BIG. Don't hold back. Fully commit yourself.

3. IF YOU DON'T A-S-K, YOU WON'T G-E-T. Ask for what you want. People will appreciate you being straight with them.

4. EMBRACE FAILURE AND REJECTION. Think of failure as an opportunity to learn. If things don't work out, figure out why. Then make some changes and try again.

5. FOCUS LESS ON YOUR IMAGE AND MORE ON WHAT YOU WANT. Do what you must to succeed without concern for your reputation or appearance.

6. PRACTICE TAKING RISKS. Pretend you have a risk-taking muscle. The more you work it, the stronger it gets.

7. DON'T BE AFRAID TO GO FIRST. Someone has to ask the first question. Someone has to be the first on the dance floor. Someone has to be the first to apologize. Someone has to say hello first. Try going first, and don't be surprised if others follow.

8. HOLD YOUR HEAD UP HIGH NO MATTER WHAT HAPPENS. If you're OK with yourself, others will be OK with you. You have permission to fail.

9. TAKE RESPONSIBLE RISKS! Don't go running across the street with your eyes closed. Don't risk your life, your safety or your life savings. Use common sense.

10. ASK YOURSELF WHAT REALLY IS AT RISK. Most of the time you have little to lose.

Well, I did give that speech and led the cheer. To my surprise, the students went along with it. It was incredible! And getting elected wasn't even the best part. The biggest reward was feeling courageous. I was so proud of myself for having taken a risk; The result almost didn't matter.

Make risk taking part of your lifestyle and I guarantee you will be a more powerful leader and more fulfilled human being.

Fire #3

BE A JUDGE, NOT A SUSPECT
Don't Worry About What Others Think – YOU Do The Thinking!

Many of us live our lives in fear of what others think of us. We worry about how others are judging us, as if they know what's best for us. It doesn't have to be that way. From this point on, you can be the judge!

Being a judge does not mean being judgmental. It will do you no good to evaluate other people or act like you're better than everyone. People deserve respect. The idea behind being a judge is that you trust your own opinions of yourself. You don't have to believe you're better than others, but you should know you're at least as good. Go with your instincts. Go with your standards. Do what you think is right. Because for you, it will be.

One student in a school band once told me she wouldn't play in a pep rally because at her school, band isn't considered cool. But doesn't she think it's cool? Doesn't the band think it's cool? Why are the band's opinions less valid than anyone else's? Each one of us can decide for ourselves what's right or acceptable.

You are a strong, creative, talented, intelligent person (especially if you've read this far in the book!). Yes, you are. You are totally qualified to decide for yourself who you want to be, and how you want to be. From now on, you get to define what's cool. Honor the real you, and you'll be the best you. Worry less about what others think, and you'll find that's when they not only like you the most, but respect you the most as well.

Instead of fitting in with others, let them try to fit in with you. Instead of giving in to peer pressure, you be the one to give peer pressure. Instead of dressing like everyone else, dress the way you want and let others copy you.

As I said in the Sandbag Chapter Seven "Pleasing Others," the most powerful you is the most authentic you. The real you is the fire.

GO FOR THE GOALS
YOU CONTROL
Do What You Can and
Forget About the Rest

Often when we fail to achieve a goal, it's not because we lack talent, ability or hard work. The problem may be the goal itself. Sometimes success or failure is out of our control. For example, let's say you aspire to win a poetry contest. You could write something absolutely beautiful, but so might another contestant. If that person wins, it's not because you've done something wrong or because of something you lack. It's because there can only be one winner, and the other contestant did something really well, totally independent of you.

There are two kinds of goals: Personal Outcomes and Personal Performances. Outcomes are results that compare you to others, such as winning a contest, getting a certain number of votes or a certain kind of recognition. Outcomes require the acknowledgement and/or participation of others. Action is required that you can't control. Personal Performances are measurements of your own effort, completely independent of outside evaluation or comparison. Performances have nothing to do with anyone else. They are all about you, and are completely within your control.

For example, an outcome goal might be to win a 10K. Your success is based on how fast other people run – something you can't control. A personal performance might be to complete the race within a certain time frame, without focus on how your time measures up to others.

Concentrating on what we can control protects us from the jealousy, insecurity and intimidation that hold us back. When we free ourselves of these worries, our performance actually improves. That's when we become most competitive. During the 2002 winter Olympics, Michelle Kwan was the favorite to win the gold medal in women's figure skating. This was a personal outcome goal, as she could not control how others skated. With this goal came significant pressure, which affected her skating. Sarah Hughes, however, never thought about the medal. She was just grateful to be competing at all. During interviews, she said all she wanted to do was skate the best she could. This was a personal performance goal – as she wasn't concerned with how she compared to others. This focus gave her the mental freedom to give a gold-medal performance.

Your control is limited to your own talent and ability. It will do you no good to aspire to out-win, out-last or out-perform others. Instead, shoot for your personal best. Limit your efforts to what you can control and don't worry about anyone else. Do that, and pretty soon you will, in fact, skate right by the competition.

FOCUS ON FACTS, NOT ON FEELINGS
How to Tell the Difference Between a Problem and Insecurity

One time I was giving a speech and I noticed a student in back of the room put her head down. I was totally insulted. Here I was doing my very best, and someone was going to sleep on me. It really upset me and I concluded that I must be doing a poor job.

When I was done, the student approached me and thanked me for my presentation. She even quoted certain messages I shared. Then she apologized. "Sorry I had my head down. I have a really bad headache. Do you have any aspirin?" I realized I had completely misinterpreted her reaction.

How many times have we all misinterpreted circumstances and felt bad for no reason? How many times have we let our insecurity affect our performance, or stop us from pursuing a goal? We humans often draw the most negative conclusions about ourselves. Sometimes we're right – things may really be pretty bad. Other times we're not right; We're insecure, and it's the voice in our head talking. So how can we tell the difference?

I use a technique called "Fact vs. Feeling." Here's how it works. If you feel bad about how something is going in your life, ask yourself if your evaluation of the situation is based on a fact, or just on your feelings. The following examples demonstrate how to do this:

Example #1: I got a 30% on a math test. I conclude I'm failing math. Is that a fact or a feeling?

Clearly it's a fact. I have statistical data to back up my conclusion. There's nothing to debate or interpret. This is a real problem.

Example #2: I see someone attractive but I conclude they'd never want to go out with me. Is that a fact or feeling?

This is a feeling. I don't really know for sure they'd reject me. My conclusion is based on fear and low self-esteem. I really have no proof to support my assumption.

If your conclusion is based on fact, you must deal with it. It's a real problem. If your conclusion is based on a feeling, there's a good chance it's merely insecurity. It might be the voice inside your head trying to hold you back. In this case, get the facts. While the voice may have been right, more often it's totally incorrect.

BEATING THE COMPETITION
How to Fly Right Past 'Em

I was on my high school debate team, which is a fiercely competitive activity. The real competition began long before debate commenced. It started the moment we'd meet our opponents. People would do all kinds of things to intimidate each other. They'd brag about previous debate victories. They'd act suspiciously calm to appear unworried. Sometimes they'd enter the room with several legal cases for transporting thousands of pages of files, evidence and documents. Often these cases contained nothing more than the person's lunch. We all played these mind games because we knew it could break our opponents down.

The best way to beat your competition is to keep them off your radar. Don't allow them to activate the insecure voice in your head. You control your own performance. Focus on what you must accomplish, do the work, and don't stop to evaluate or compare yourself to others.

I'll never forget the day I arrived to run the Los Angeles Marathon. I freaked out at seeing thousands of "athletes." Everyone seemed so comfortable and experienced. They laughed, talked about their training and compared running shoes. It was totally intimidating. I felt like such an outsider. There was no way I could compete with them – or so I thought. To my delight (and complete shock), I passed up two thirds of them along the way. I sometimes wonder if I could have done even better had I not freaked myself out at the beginning.

It's easy to give up on goals or underestimate your chances of achieving them when there's a lot of competition. The cynical voice in our head likes to remind us that the odds are against us. It points out every advantage our competitors have and where we lack. When there's a lot of competition, we start doing the math and conclude our chances of winning are slim.

Competition is less about "odds" and more about our state of mind. The key isn't to do better than others. It's to get in a state of mind that makes other people's performance irrelevant.

If you can persevere and perform at 100 percent, you'll give yourself an edge over others. You're more qualified than you think. And while all of us fail some of the time, we also can and do succeed. If it's possible, at some point it's probable.

Most of your competition is equally insecure and will give up early. The longer you stick with it, the better your chances. You're closer to success with every attempt. So don't worry about anyone else. Be the best you possible and the competition will beat itself.

SET YOUR SIGHTS
ON YOUR STRENGTHS
Let Your Greatness Lift You Up

I'll never forget my fifth grade teacher, Ms. Peterson. (Named changed to protect the guilty!) On the first day of school, Ms. Peterson announced, "Today, you all have an A!" We were thrilled, until we realized what she was actually saying. From that point on, she was going to subtract points. She was going to look for our mistakes and weaknesses. She graded our papers with a red pen and marked the margins with criticism. The more red ink we had on our returned papers, the worse we felt. Sure, the red alerted us to where we needed to work harder. But for many students, it slowly chipped away at their self-esteem. Ms. Peterson meant well, but her critical approach to instruction did less to teach us, and more to make us feel bad about school.

Not all my teachers were like that. In high school, Mr. Harvey taught physics. Unlike Ms. Peterson, he looked for opportunities to praise us. He'd give us points for asking intelligent questions. He'd give us partial credit when our answers on a test were "sort of" right. One time I mistakenly erased a correct answer after second-guessing myself. When he graded my test, he could read my erasure mark and gave me two points for having good first instincts.

With both teachers I was always aware of what I did right and what I did wrong. Both teachers wanted me to improve. But by emphasizing what I was doing well, Mr. Harvey kept my confidence up. That made it easier to learn.

Ultimately we are responsible for our own learning and growth. We can improve ourselves in two ways: enhance our strengths and improve on our weaknesses. Your time is best spent focused on your strengths. Our strengths distinguish us and make us unique. They are what we are remembered for. We all have weaknesses, but our strengths outweigh them.

Many people fixate on what's wrong with them. They think they can't move forward unless they correct their shortcomings. History shows this just isn't true. People have always succeeded, in spite of weaknesses. If Michael Jordan spent his life focusing on improving his baseball skills, he may never have developed into the basketball legend he has become. He went with his strengths, and it's those for which we remember him.

You may not have the looks and abilities you'd like. But, you have other qualities and talents that will enable you to achieve greatness. Your imperfections are like the holes in Swiss cheese. We enjoy the cheese and don't worry about the holes.

To be successful, you don't need to be good at all things. You just have to be great at one. Avoid putting unnecessary pressure on yourself. Don't ignore areas where you need to improve, but spend most of your energy working on the things where you have potential to be great. Set your sights on your strengths. They are a fire that will lift you to success, even if you carry a few sandbags of weakness along with you.

TAKE IT AS IT COMES
Letting Your Life Unfold

There's an ancient Tibetan story about a wise old farmer. One day his one and only horse ran away. The neighbors cried for him and mourned the tribulations of life. He merely responded, "How do we know what's good or bad?" It's a good question, as circumstances are hard to interpret. Well, his luck changed. A week later, the horse returned, accompanied by two handsome stallions. The neighbors rejoiced at the farmer's good fortune. His response was the same as before: "How do we know what's good or bad?" A few days later his son climbs on one of the new horses to train him. The horse throws him and he breaks his leg. Again the neighbors come to console the old man. His response is always the same. "How do we know what's good or bad?" A few months go by and the military recruiter comes for the old farmer's son, as all healthy young men must report for duty. However, because of his leg injury, he is pardoned from fighting. And on and on the story goes.

When we isolate any one experience it's easy to lose perspective. Over the course of time, our experiences take on new meaning. What hurts today may benefit you tomorrow. What feels great today may have consequences later.

I can testify to this from my life. While going to film school, I was diagnosed with cancer, which felt bad. That experience eventually led me to change careers and I became a speaker, which was wonderful. But speaking has meant a lot of time away from home, which can be difficult. Being away from home has allowed me to visit a lot of new places and make a lot of great friends. I have no doubt my life will continue to ebb and flow in this pattern.

We're better off not evaluating everything that happens to us. Instead, just let things happen, and trust that every experience enriches our lives and moves us along our path. Enjoy the good times while you have them, and trust that something wonderful may come from the difficult times.

FINDING WHAT'S IN IT FOR YOU
Be a Student, Not a Victim

The expression "What's in it for me?" is typically characterized as a selfish statement. It implies that to do something, there must be a benefit to you. Selfishness usually comes from fear. We're afraid that if we take care of others first, our needs won't be met. Fortunately, many of us have learned that taking care of others IS the best way to get our needs met.

Still, the question "What's in it for me?" can be quite useful. Sometimes we're forced into situations we don't want to be in. Other times we fail, we lose or we get rejected. If you find yourself in one of these situations, try asking yourself "What's in it for me?" Often, you actually get an answer. Sometimes there are pearls of wisdom to be discovered in our painful moments. What we interpret as a negative situation could also be a gift, depending on how wide your eyes are open.

When I was diagnosed with cancer at age 22, it was tragic and scary. But I remembered the messages of speakers I had heard in school. Many of them had overcome great adversity. One guy was imprisoned in a POW camp in Vietnam. Another had very short arms and an artificial leg. Rather than feel sorry for themselves, these guys remained positive. Not only did they overcome their challenges, they learned from them, acquiring so much wisdom that now people pay them to hear it.

I had forgotten all about these guys until my diagnosis. Their messages must have been waiting in the back of my brain, knowing this day might come. So I thought, "What if the cancer doesn't kill me? What's if it's just a life experience like those speaker guys back in high school? Imagine the lessons I could learn!"

That approach to my illness – coming at it as a student rather than a victim – was quite powerful. It gave me strength, and it opened me up to the rich wisdom that comes from a difficult experience. I learned the value of life and the power of attitude. I learned about fear and how it clouds our thinking. Most importantly, I learned how strong I was (and how strong we all are). This illness was not a tragedy. It was a gift. There was something in it for me. While I wouldn't want to repeat the experience, I'm grateful for having had it.

There are also lessons to be learned in your challenges. There's something in them for you. Embrace every experience and mine it for all it's worth. Avoid judging your circumstance. Just have the experience, and keep your eyes and ears open. I promise something in there will make you a little smarter, and a little stronger.

EARNING RESPECT
Live With Honor and Influence

Many people put in a leadership position assume their title will win the respect and loyalty of others. They quickly learn that title alone will not do the trick. Think about how many people have been put in charge of you that you didn't respect. If you're a leader, you must win others' loyalty. Who are the people you respect? What about them are you responding to? I have found that effective, admired leaders demonstrate many of the following qualities:

HONESTY: People appreciate the truth.

TRUST: People will respect you if they know they can count on you, and if they feel you will count on them.

RELIABILITY: No one likes a flake.

HONOR: No one can condemn you for doing what's right.

INTEGRITY: Be true to yourself and what you believe in.

KINDNESS: Treat others with care.

CONFIDENCE: We believe in people who believe in themselves.

VISION: Give your followers something to believe in.

A PLAN: Know how to make positive change.

SUCCESS: People notice how you behave and what you achieve.

PUBLIC SPEAKING SKILLS: To motivate, you must be able to communicate.

LISTENING SKILLS: People want to know they'll be heard.

COMMITMENT: If you're willing to hang in there until the job is done, so will your followers.

The more of these qualities you have, the more people will want to follow your lead. They'll not only be willing, they'll be honored.

LIVING IN THE NOW
The Power of Presence

When I was a kid my mom used to call me a worrywart. I constantly stressed out over what might happen. What if the school bus doesn't come? What if the older kids at school pick on me? In seventh grade I almost gave myself a heart attack in pre-algebra, because if I didn't do well, then in eighth grade I wouldn't be in algebra, which meant in ninth grade I wouldn't be in geometry, which meant in 10th grade I wouldn't be in Algebra II/Trig, which meant in 11th grade I wouldn't be in pre-calculus, which meant I couldn't take senior year calculus, and then no good college would want me, which meant I was destined to be mediocre and poor. I really thought this in seventh grade! By obsessing on my distant future, I wasn't able to just enjoy junior high.

Most of us are more ambitious about the future than we are the present. We let our worries stop us from fully experiencing today. We allow our minds to wander. We do one thing while thinking about the next thing we have to do. We stress over what we'll do if the worst thing happens. The more time we spend thinking about sometime or someplace else, the less time we spend right here, right now. How much of your life have you missed out on by not being present?

While it's important to set goals and prepare for the future, ultimately we need to focus on our current physical location. That's where we have most control. The present is something real, whereas the future is based on an unreliable prediction. One way to refocus on the present is to ask yourself questions that will pull you back. What do you notice about right now? How is your body feeling? Where are you? Who are you with? What's going on around you? Answering these questions requires experiencing the present.

Well, I did get into algebra, but by the time my senior year rolled around, I chose not to take calculus. I still got into a pretty good college, and although I had a great experience there, my ability to make a living today has little to do with the status of my college. My seventh grade worries did nothing but stop me from enjoying those days.

I've learned that not only can we not predict the future, but we can't even predict what we're going to want when that future comes. I've also learned that tomorrow is a byproduct of today. So be present in every moment. The future will take care of itself.

ASKING FOR WHAT YOU WANT
If You Don't A-S-K, You Won't G-E-T

One time I was waiting for my order at a photocopy store. Their machine was jammed, so it was taking a long time to complete my job. Wanting to be productive, I asked a clerk if I could use their phone to make a local call. She said no. I felt a little put off.

Eager to make my call, I decided to alter my approach. I found another clerk and changed the wording of my question. "Excuse me, I need to make a local call. Which phone is best for me to use?" I was immediately shown to a desk. Feeling empowered, I then took it a step further. "Excuse me, I've been waiting a while and I need to get back to my office. How soon can you have someone deliver the job?" They agreed to bring it to my office the moment it was done. And since they were making me wait (as I reminded them in my question), implicitly there would be no charge for this service.

I've learned that our specific wording of requests is critical to getting what we want. In the first instance I empowered the clerk with a close-ended question (meaning yes or no) about permission: "Is there a phone I can use?" Asking the question this way implies that "no" is a possible answer. To end the situation, all the clerk has to do is shake her head. That's very easy for her. In my second attempt, I consciously moved beyond the permission stage, establishing my presumption that it would be OK, and all I needed to know was which phone I should use. To the second clerk, it's much more difficult to say "no" because this time it would require an explanation and confrontation. The most comfortable response is to grant my request.

People often opt for the easiest way out. They prefer to avoid confrontation. So when you make a request, start from a place that assumes the person is willing to help. Don't ask for permission; ask for options. Obviously you should respect their wishes. If it's really a problem, they'll let you know. Be sure you honor that. Still, it never hurts to ask. You'll be surprised by how often they'll accommodate you.

CONNECTING THROUGH KINDNESS
Give Out What You Want Back

We've all heard the expression "It's not what you know, it's who you know." But knowing people is not enough. It's taking care of people that comes back to you. The more kindness you send out, the more it will come back to you.

My sophomore year of high school I moved to a new school. There were 2,000 students and I knew no one. For the first two weeks it was unbelievably lonely. I could handle not knowing anyone in class, but during breaks it was brutal. I was so self-conscious about being alone I use to walk around campus during lunch pretending I had things to do. The truth is, I just didn't want anyone to see me sitting alone.

One day this familiar looking guy came up to me and asked, "Aren't you in my P.E. class?" I realized that's where I knew him from, so I nodded my head. He extended his hand and said, "Hi, I'm Mike." I was never alone again at school.

It was such a small gesture for him. For me it was life changing. Years later we had dinner together in Arizona. He really didn't remember what he did. I never forgot. And when the check came, I was happy to pick it up. I would do anything for Mike.

You never know how or if your kindness will be remembered. The kinder you are, the more it comes back to you. People do return favors. More importantly, it's empowering. When you do something for someone else, it takes your mind off your own problems. It raises your self-image and, well, it just plain feels good. If you feel bad about yourself, try doing something kind for someone else. Then watch how quickly you begin to feel better. Talk to anyone who does a lot of community service and they'll tell you it's unbelievably addictive.

One holiday season I volunteered to pack food bags for needy families. When I arrived at the packing facility, there were hundreds of people there, all wanting to make a difference. Outside on the streets of Los Angeles, none of these people might have ever spoken to each other. But by coming together to do something kind, it brought out the kindness in everyone. It was the most friendly gathering I've ever been to. It was a wonderful opportunity to meet new people and make new friends.

The best way to network is to look for opportunities to help others. Do this without thought about how it will come back to help you. Just look for ways to help other people accomplish their goals and be who they want to be. Be spreading your kindness, you expand your personal network. That can only be good for you.

Share your heart. Share your money. Share your food. Share you. Think in terms of the "we," and you'll never have to worry about the "me."

HELP!
If There's a Wolf, Cry Wolf!

Many people feel that to be smart, strong or sane, they must manage their problems alone. To many, seeking help is a sign of weakness. I'm amazed by how many young people I talk to who have very real problems, but are afraid to tell their parents or a counselor. They put on a happy face, but struggle inside. For some of these people, their image is more important than their inner peace or their physical health. For others, it's pure denial. They believe that as long as they don't acknowledge their problem, it's not really there.

One of the most courageous things you can do is to admit when you need help. That's the first step to improvement. Whether you want to overcome a problem or achieve a goal, all around you are incredible human resources who can help. Successful people rely on these resources. Tiger Woods has a coach and consults his caddy for club selections and the best way to approach the hole. U.S. presidents use advisors. Celebrities work with acting coaches. Professional speakers use speech coaches (myself included). Millions of people consult therapists and counselors to work through emotional and psychological challenges. This doesn't make them crazy. If they're unhappy, they'd be crazy NOT to talk to someone.

Don't be shy about building a team of people to set you up for success. Use your parents, teachers, coaches, counselors and tutors. Call hotlines, visit Web sites or join a support group. If you have a physical problem, talk to a doctor. Don't worry about how people will respond or how you will look. Don't think you're overreacting. Getting help doesn't mean you're weak. It means you're smart.

SIX STEPS TO KEEP YOURSELF MOTIVATED
Keep the Fire Lit

Most of us suffer from "Good Intention Syndrome," a condition where we have a great goal but always seem to have a reason to delay pursuing it. There really is NO reason not to get working on your goals. The trick is to muster up discipline to put you in motion. Here are some ideas to give you a jump-start:

1. Set deadlines for tasks and don't allow yourself to miss them.

2. Ask yourself what's the most important thing you could be doing at any given moment. Work on top priorities.

3. Remind yourself how your life will improve when this goal is achieved.

4. Talk about your goal regularly to other people to keep yourself focused. (This helped me train for the L.A. Marathon. It also put pressure on me to train so I wouldn't embarrass myself by giving up.)

5. Dedicate a specific, uninterrupted time during the day to work on your goal. NEVER violate this time.

6. If nothing else, devote 12 minutes a day toward your goal. If you do this five days a week, it'll add up to four hours a month. After a few months, you WILL SEE RESULTS.

FINAL THOUGHTS

Well, there's the information. I'll bet a lot of it you already knew. Rarely are we held back by a lack of knowledge or ideas. Usually the issue is more about courage and follow-through.

The burden is now on you to take action. Consider what ideas you had while reading this book. Surely something popped into your head. You are strong. You are powerful. Trust yourself to be successful. And start today. Do the things you must to expose your capable inner self. Cut loose your sandbags. Let your fire – your burning desire to succeed – lift you up toward your goals. They're up there waiting for you.

May something you've read in these pages help you soar. Take flight today.

Scott Greenberg